Do not be conformed to this world, but be transformed by the renewal of your mind, that by testing you may discern what is the will of God, what is good and acceptable and perfect.

ROMANS 12:2 ESV

TRANSFORM

TRANSFORMED BY OUR ENCOUNTER WITH JESUS

SCOTT MICHAEL RINGO

OCEAN GRAND

To my family, my parents, and grandparents who taught me of Jesus' love for me and modeled an example of believers in community changing the world.

Transformed by Our Encounter with Jesus

Six lessons designed to systematically take you, a group of friends, or a small group through their transformation in Christ and then as an individual, a family, or a small group engage in transforming the surrounding community.

Cover design and book formatting by Scott and Tristan Ringo

TRANSFORM

Published by Ocean Grand

Virginia Beach, Virginia

Copyright © 2008 by Scott Michael Ringo

All rights reserved.

Cover Design: Scott Michael Ringo

Photo: Shutterstock

First Edition 2008

Printed in the United States of America.

No part of this book may be reproduced in any form or by any electronic or mechanical means, including information storage and retrieval systems, without written permission from the author, except for the use of brief quotations in a book review.

Permissions

Scripture quotations are from the ESV® Bible (The Holy Bible, English Standard Version®), copyright © 2001 by Crossway, a publishing ministry of Good News Publishers. Used by permission. All rights reserved.

Character Building Questions adapted from, Neal Cole, "Cultivating a life for God: Multiplying Disciples" (Carrol Stream, IL : Church Smart Resources, 1999). Used by permission. All rights reserved.

This study is to be used for Bible study by individuals within a group. No portion of this document or design may be reproduced, stored in a retrieval system, or transmitted in any form outside of its intended use without written permission.

All emphasis in Scripture quotations has been added by the author.

ISBN 978-1-7356637-0-8

eISBN 978-1-7356637-1-5

CONTENTS

How to use this book	ix
Introduction	xv
LESSON I Marks of a True Christian	1
LESSON II Actions Speak Louder Than Words	15
LESSON III Equipped	33
LESSON IV Transforming Our Communities	53
LESSON V Our Job of Evangelism	71
LESSON VI Unity	91
Appendix	113
Character Building Questions	115
Accepting Jesus	117
Epilogue	120
Notes	123
About the Author	125
Titles by Scott Michael Ringo	127

HOW TO USE THIS BOOK

LEADER INTRODUCTION

What would it look like if a ragtag group of people had a genuine encounter with Jesus, could learn His ways, and then He sent them out into the world to transform history? You might think that question was referring to the twelve disciples that Jesus mentored. Yet, we know their story and the impact they had on the world because if you know Jesus; it was because of them you know Him. Instead, the question refers to another ragtag group of people, the ones that makeup you and your friends, your family, or even the small group of believers you are a part of. Why are you, your family, or your small group of friends any different from the original disciples and the impact they had on the world? The fact is, there should not be any difference in you or the disciples and the impact they had on the world. Both sets of disciples met and know Jesus. Both sets of disciples have the same instruction, equipping, gifting, Holy Spirit, and mandate to make disciples. You, your family, or group only need to believe they can change the world like the first. Ride along and bring your ragtag group on a journey that could change the face of your church, your city, or even the world. We dare you to take the journey.

This book can guide you, a family, a group of friends, or a small group in their transformation in Christ. Second, to engage you or that group of people as you transform the surrounding community. Many times our family time or even our weekly small group meetings become only another event to attend. If we are honest, like attending church, our weekly attendance does not reproduce disciples. The real benefit of a family or group of friends is you have people committed to each other that could be the catalyst to transforming your community for Jesus. This book will take you through discovering what being a true follower of Jesus looks like and then how to affect your community in an ongoing, real, and tangible way. Through this book, you, your family or group of friends can get excited about what Jesus has called you to do daily and begin putting your faith into action.

HOW TO USE THIS BOOK

This discovery can be as easy or as intense as you would like to make it. Below explains each lesson and how it can be best used to see your family or group transformed into a force that can transform your community. Being Christians is much more than attending church once a week and a small group study one other night of the week. As we will see in the example of the early church, their transformation in Christ transformed their community and eventually the world.

This might be the first week you have thought about getting your family, group of friends, or your small group together. This might be a transformation you need to go through alone. Or maybe your family or group of friends are seasoned veterans

HOW TO USE THIS BOOK

of living life together and making a difference of those you know. Either way, I designed this guide to affect and lead the new Christian and the longtime believer in a deeper discovery of God's role and plan for their life.

This guide is designed to give you and your group all the pieces for transformation as a group through impacting your community and those you encounter. But, if you are an individual, this study can stand on its own and self-lead you through making a significant impact in your community and those you encounter while waiting for other believers to join you.

MEETING TOGETHER

Even if you are going through this alone, at some point you might get an idea of who you might take through this discovery process. You might have already figured out how and when your family or group of friends will get together and talk through the lessons. This might be something you study with friends at a coffee shop, others at work, your family at home, or a small group at your church. Each different type of group you build with this has the potential to transform your community and the people you experience differently.

THE FIRST WEEK

Discussion questions are included with each lesson designed for the group, and there are extra sections in the "Next Steps" that may be best for the individual to study on their own. There are no apologies that this study asks the participant some hard questions about themselves considering the weekly Bible passages. You want your group to wrestle, without reservations, with the truths in the Bible. Review with your group which sections are which, so they can fully engage the study.

HOW TO USE THIS BOOK

GROUP HOMEWORK AND GROUP ACTIVITIES

Woven into the study are homework and activities to help your group apply the passages to their own lives. These are optional, but those in your group may never have a better opportunity to apply what they learn better than taking the extra time as a group and seeing how amazing it is to get involved with transforming their communities.

We hope that this Bible study cultivates many rich things in your group as you move through the study. By wrestling together through the way God wants to transform our lives and community can be messy but, it is worth it to see our lives transformed by Jesus.

THE DIFFERENT SECTIONS OF EACH LESSON

Each week of the "Transform" study has about eight sections. I design each section specifically to help your group study, discuss, and apply the study to their own lives. Below explains the sections and how you might use them.

Scripture

Each week of the study there is a scripture that is a chapter or several verses out of a chapter(s). All the scripture is included in the study so that the study can be done from this book, which makes it convenient for traveling, or hiking, or wherever you are. All you need to build a group of community transforming believers is a copy of this book. We encourage people to read along from their own Bibles or other translations if desired. Encourage your group to read the scripture part of each lesson before to your group getting together or getting online to talk through it. When your group gets together go around the room

HOW TO USE THIS BOOK

and read the Bible part again before diving into the discussion questions so it is fresh in everyone's mind.

Quick Notes

The quick notes is a section that may help people understand the scriptures better. They are a summary of each of the corresponding sections of the Bible passages. There are some extra notes in the Quick notes to help explain the passage.

Discussion

The Discussion section is where your group interacts with each other about the Bible passages. The questions can take your group through the three levels of communication from what they know, what they think, and finally who they are, developing additional levels of relationship with each other. Go through the discussion questions within your group for each lesson.

Next Steps

The Next Steps section is for each individual to work through in the days after the lesson. They are deep and pointed questions that help a person apply the lesson to their individual life. When we read something in the Bible that is there to make our Christian walk better we should be quick to apply it to our own lives. As your group works through the "Next Steps" section each week on their own and listens to what God is saying to them, they can have a better understanding and finish that week out with a powerful application of the lesson. This section need not be shared with the group; it is between them and God.

HOW TO USE THIS BOOK

Prayer Points

The prayer points are for your group to pray through together at the end of the night. It is a good way to pray that God helps apply the lesson in your groups' lives. Remember to ask for other prayer requests specific to the group, write those down, and pray through them for the week.

Group Homework

The Group Homework section is just that, homework that each person in your group takes home, works through, and then brings back to discuss at the beginning of the next week's discussion. It is a way for your group to apply the lesson throughout the week and then recap it the next week. It helps bring growth and continuity to your study together. Be sure to read ahead as a leader in your studies and activities. Several of the activities are involved, so be prepared to walk your group through these activities.

Journal

At the end of each lesson are journal pages. Journaling is a great way to hear Jesus in what we are learning. It is also a great way to keep a diary of notes, thoughts, and action steps from the lesson. Once the study is finished and the pages filled out, it is a great resource to return to time and time again as we take action to transform our communities. I highly encourage you to take time and listen to Jesus and fill up the journal pages. If you are reading this in an electronic format, you can make digital notes right in the application.

INTRODUCTION

Transform is a word that encompasses the gospel of the Bible, yet it may be the hardest concept for us, as Christians, to manifest daily. For many of us, we know Jesus has transformed our lives, yet the continual transformation is a daily, even hourly process. In this study, we are going to look at what the Bible says about how our own lives should look like Jesus' and then how we need to respond to it in our communities.

> **transform** |trans fôrm| verb [trans.] make a thorough or dramatic change in the form, appearance, or character of [1]

As the gospel engages our life, perhaps the question we should ask ourselves is whether we are open to transformation. First, we must change into the likeness of Christ, and then we will be someone that Christ can use to help others find His transforming power. Another way to look at this is when a budding student wants to be a doctor they have to go to medical school, apply themselves and allow the professors and doctors they intern under transform them into doctors. Merely wanting

INTRODUCTION

to be a doctor does not make one a doctor. Neither does going to medical school without applying themselves or opposing the information learned. Once they apply themselves, learn the information, and pass the exams they become like the professors and doctors they learned from. They can then go on and help others with their medical knowledge and skill.

The significant news about the gospel, as we will learn, does not require us to attend years and years of schooling in order that our lives change into something that Christ can use. Instead, the largest part of how we are transformed comes the instant we accept Jesus, and our part is to yield to the transforming power of Christ. At the beginning of this book is a good place to make sure you and/or anyone going through it know and accept Jesus Christ as the Messiah. In the Appendix of this book are a few pages that share the simple gospel message and how to accept Jesus as savior. Turn to the *Appendix, Accepting Jesus* pages and read through it. This is a great time to make sure everyone knows the gospel and Jesus. Once we do that, Jesus uses us to show his image to those around us and the world. We can also call this apprenticeship or discipleship. The original twelve disciples were apprentices of Jesus for three years. They lived, traveled, ate, and slept with Jesus. You may surprise you to hear, merely wanting to be a disciple of Jesus' does not make one a disciple. To be a disciple, we must follow Jesus, apply the biblical truths of the Bible to our lives, and be obedient to Jesus' commandments to be His disciple. It is easy, but like the early disciples following Jesus, we must take the first step.

One of the most amazing things about how God has chosen our role in His plan is the responsibility He has given us in the scheme of things. If the world is going to see Christ, then they are going to see it through our lives. Christ came to earth and lived a simple life as a man. While He was here on the earth for

33 years His entire purpose was to show men His Father God. Everything He did was to point mankind to Father God. Likewise, when Christ returned to heaven, He gave us that exact mandate. We are to allow Him to transform our lives so we are just like Him and our purpose is to show mankind Father God. We are to make disciples.

If mankind is going to know Jesus, God, and the Holy Spirit, they depend on us who know Him to introduce them. That is an incredible responsibility that Jesus left for us to finish. Part of allowing Jesus to transform our lives is to change us to be like Him and then to share the message of the gospel, introducing them to Jesus so they can receive Jesus' transformation. The role of discipleship is now our mission, just as it was the original twelve disciples. We must meet Jesus, allow him to transform us, follow Him so we know Him and make disciples of others.

One of God's promises to mankind in Matthew 24 says,

> "And this gospel of the kingdom will be proclaimed throughout the whole world as a testimony to all nations, and then the end will come" (Matthew 24:14 ESV).[2]

It is clear from this verse that we share the gospel throughout the world before the end comes and Jesus comes to take us home. Starting in Genesis chapter 10, there is evidence that God's mission includes people of all nations, tongues, and tribes. Genesis chapter 10, lists seventy nations which God promises to bless through Abraham in Genesis 12:1-3. It is our mandate as Christians to take this gospel to the world by action, deed, example, and word. Just before ascending into heaven He left us in charge of making sure this happens when He said,

INTRODUCTION

> All authority in heaven and on earth has been given to me. Go therefore and make disciples of all nations, baptizing them in the name of the Father and of the Son and of the Holy Spirit, teaching them to observe all that I have commanded you. And behold, I am with you always, to the end of the age (Matthew 28:18-20).

Once we are believers with transformed lives, our mission is to make disciples, baptizing them, and teaching them all that Jesus taught us. Have you ever wondered about the purpose for your life? Here in these three verses is the answer. The only thing left to decide is are we going to obey and spend our lives making disciples? The question that remains is will we be obedient to Jesus to take the gospel to our friends, Co-workers, neighbors, and world so that the entire world will have the chance to know Jesus before He comes back?

1
MARKS OF A TRUE CHRISTIAN

ONE
MARKS OF A TRUE CHRISTIAN

Romans 12:1-21

A Living Sacrifice

1 I appeal to you therefore, brothers, by the mercies of God, to present your bodies as a living sacrifice, holy and acceptable to God, which is your spiritual worship. 2 Do not be conformed to this world, but be transformed by the renewal of your mind, that by testing you may discern what is the will of God, what is good and acceptable and perfect.

Gifts of Grace

3 For by the grace given to me I say to everyone among you not to think of himself more highly than he ought to think, but to think with sober judgment, each according to the measure of faith that God has assigned. 4 For as in one body we have many members, and the members do not all have the same function, 5 so we, though many, are one body in Christ, and individually members one of another. 6 Having gifts that differ according to the grace given to us, let

us use them: if prophecy, in proportion to our faith; 7 if service, in our serving; the one who teaches, in his teaching; 8 the one who exhorts, in his exhortation; the one who contributes, in generosity; the one who leads, with zeal; the one who does acts of mercy, with cheerfulness.

Marks of the True Christian

9 Let love be genuine. Abhor what is evil; hold fast to what is good. 10 Love one another with brotherly affection. Outdo one another in showing honor. 11 Do not be slothful in zeal, be fervent in spirit, serve the Lord. 12 Rejoice in hope, be patient in tribulation, be constant in prayer. 13 Contribute to the needs of the saints and seek to show hospitality.

14 Bless those who persecute you; bless and do not curse them. 15 Rejoice with those who rejoice, weep with those who weep. 16 Live in harmony with one another. Do not be haughty, but associate with the lowly. Never be conceited. 17 Repay no one evil for evil, but give thought to do what is honorable in the sight of all. 18 If possible, so far as it depends on you, live peaceably with all. 19 Beloved, never avenge yourselves, but leave

it to the wrath of God, for it is written, 'Vengeance is mine, I will repay, says the Lord.' 20 To the contrary, 'if your enemy is hungry, feed him; if he is thirsty, give him something to drink; for by so doing you will heap burning coals on his head.' 21 Do not be overcome by evil, but overcome evil with good (Romans 12:1-21).

lesson one quick notes

Paul wrote Romans about AD 57, or about twenty-four years after Jesus died on the cross and rose again. Paul wrote Romans to the believers who lived in Rome. Paul packs Romans full of instructions on how to live the Christian life to its fullest. Romans is also a book that, unless you live by faith and grace, is hard to live up to as a Christian.

Romans 12:1-2

Paul urges Christians to give their lives to God as a sacrifice. Since they are living beings the sacrifice is their lives and bodies in such a way that it is acceptable to God. Paul reminds them to not be tied or molded to this world but to allow Christ to transform them by renewing their minds. He reminds us that it is through testing that we are able to discern God's will and know what is acceptable in our lives for Him.

Romans 12:3-8

Paul reminds us that we are to remember humility and when we deal with each other no one is more important than the other. Every one of us as Christians is important. Though we are not all the same in how God has gifted us, each of us has a necessary piece of the puzzle, and we should encourage each other to use those gifts.

Romans 12:9-21

Work so that your love is true, dislike what is evil, and like what is good. Care, love, and honor each other. These twelve verses are key in what makes us as believers more like Christ. It is obeying passages of scripture like these that steer us completely opposite of the world. We see in these verses that God speaks first to how we should be and then continues on to explain how we should be to others. He ends this passage making sure that we understand we are to love even our enemies and let them see only love from us.

lesson one discussion

As Christians, we are to be and act very different from the rest of the world. There are influences every day in our lives that try to teach us how we should be as humans, but the Bible is supposed to be our guide, not the world. In Romans 12:1-21, Paul explains to us in plain English exactly how we are to act towards others, and we are to do that as a living sacrifice to God. In these verses, there is little to guess at. Paul is very clear what are the marks of a true Christian. What of these attributes do you need to work on to be a better picture of Christ?

- Go around the room and each person share a person they have dreamed of being. What about them makes you want to be them?

- What do you think Paul means when he says, "to present your bodies as a living sacrifice, holy and acceptable to God, which is your spiritual worship?" Does he literally mean we are to sacrifice ourselves?

- Which of the characteristics of a Christian do you think is the hardest to develop, and why? Each person discuss his or her challenge.

- How do you feel when a Christian treat you in a way contrary to the way Paul describes we are to treat others? Why do you feel that way?

- Who is someone that comes to mind in your life

when you read verses 19-21 where Paul is talking about loving your enemy? Is there someone right now in your life you might consider an enemy? Each person name someone that comes to mind.

- How can you make a step towards loving that person that you might consider an enemy? How do you think it will make them feel when loved by you?

lesson one next steps

When we read about a truth in the Bible that will make our Christian walk better should we jump at the opportunity and immediately apply it to our own lives. Work through the steps below to apply the truths in this lesson to your own life. You need not share this with the group; it is between you and God.

- Do I allow myself to conform to this world?

- Am I able to discern the will of God in my life? If not, what are some things that may keep me from doing that?

- Do I exalt myself as though I am better than others? What does Paul say about this in this passage?

- What are my spiritual gifts? Do I know what they are? (If not, take a spiritual gifts test)

- Is my love for others genuine? Do I honor others by loving them? If not, what can I do to change this?

- Who do I consider my enemy? What can I do this week to show love toward someone I have a problem loving?

Flip to the Appendix and answer the Character-Building Questions.

lesson one prayer points

- Pray that those in your group will have greater strength to resist conforming to this world.

- Greater love for everyone, including your enemies

- That God would show you one person who you might consider your enemy and start putting a plan together to love them.

Other Group Prayer Needs:

lesson one group homework

Finish this page for next week's study and bring your work with you to the group.

- Who were the people that came to mind in your life when you read Romans 19-21 where Paul is talking about loving your enemy?

- How did you make a step towards loving each of those people listed above?

- How did it make them feel when loved by you?

Memorize this passage:

> I appeal to you therefore, brothers, by the mercies of God, to present your bodies as a living sacrifice, holy and acceptable to God, which is your spiritual worship. Do not be conformed to this world, but be transformed by the renewal of your mind, that by testing you may discern what is the will of God, what is good and acceptable and perfect (Romans 12:1&2).

Journal Pages

This is a great opportunity to journal what you are learning or the action steps you want to take based on this lesson. Doing so will keep all your notes and journaling in this book as future reference. Start by taking a few minutes to pray and ask Jesus to bring to light all you are learning and what transformational changes you can make in your life. If you are reading this in an electronic version, make a digital note and journal.

Journal Pages

II
ACTIONS SPEAK LOUDER THAN WORDS

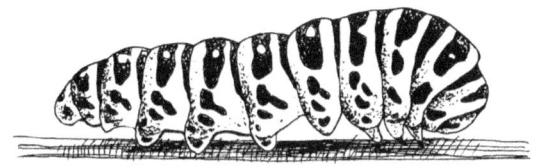

TWO
ACTIONS SPEAK LOUDER THAN WORDS

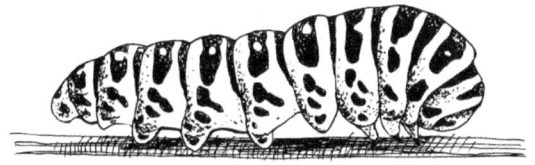

James 2:1-26 & Matt 25:31-46

The Sin of Partiality

1 My brothers, show no partiality as you hold the faith in our Lord Jesus Christ, the Lord of glory. 2 For if a man wearing a gold ring and fine clothing comes into your assembly, and a poor man in shabby clothing also comes in, 3 and if you pay attention to the one who wears the fine clothing and say, "You sit here in a good place," while you say to the poor man, "You stand over there," or, "Sit down at my feet," 4 have you not then made distinctions among yourselves and become judges with evil thoughts? 5 Listen, my beloved brothers, has not God chosen those who are poor in the world to be rich in faith and heirs of the kingdom, which he has promised to those who love him? 6 But you have dishonored the poor man. Are not the rich the ones who oppress you, and the ones who drag you into court?

7 Are they not the ones who blaspheme the honorable name by which you were called?

8 If you really fulfill the royal law according to the Scripture, "You shall love your neighbor as yourself," you are doing well. 9 But if you show partiality, you are committing sin and are convicted by the law as transgressors. 10 For whoever keeps the whole law but fails in one point has become guilty of all of it. 11 For he who said, "Do not commit adultery," also said, "Do not murder." If you do not commit adultery but do murder, you have become a transgressor of the law. 12 So speak and so act as those who are to be judged under the law of liberty. 13 For judgment is without mercy to one who has shown no mercy. Mercy triumphs over judgment.

Faith Without Works Is Dead

14 What good is it, my brothers, if someone says he has faith but does not have works? Can that faith save him? 15 If a brother or sister is poorly clothed and lacking in daily food, 16 and one of you says to them, "Go in peace, be warmed and filled," without giving them the things needed for the body, what good is that? 17 So also faith by itself, if it does not have works, is dead.

18 But someone will say, "You have faith and I have works." Show me your faith apart from your works, and I will show you my faith by my works. 19 You believe that God is one; you do well. Even the demons believe—and shudder! 20 Do you want to be shown, you foolish person, that faith apart from works is useless? 21 Was not Abraham our father justified by works when he offered up his son Isaac on the altar? 22 You see that faith was active along with his works, and faith was completed by his works; 23 and the Scripture was fulfilled that says, "Abraham believed God, and it was counted to him as righteousness"—

and he was called a friend of God. 24 You see that a person is justified by works and not by faith alone. 25 And in the same way was not also Rahab the prostitute justified by works when she received the messengers and sent them out by another way? 26 For as the body apart from the spirit is dead, so also faith apart from works is dead. (James 2:1-26).

The Final Judgment

31 When the Son of Man comes in his glory, and all the angels with him, then he will sit on his glorious throne. 32 Before him will be gathered all the nations, and he will separate people one from another as a shepherd separates the sheep from the goats. 33 And he will place the sheep on his right, but the goats on the left. 34 Then the King will say to those on his right, 'Come, you who are blessed by my Father, inherit the kingdom prepared for you from the foundation of the world. 35 For I was hungry and you gave me food, I was thirsty and you gave me drink, I was a stranger and you welcomed me, 36 I was naked and you clothed me, I was sick and you visited me, I was in prison and you came to me.' 37 Then the righteous will answer him, saying, 'Lord, when did we see you hungry and feed you, or thirsty and give you drink? 38 And when did we see you a stranger and welcome you, or naked and clothe you? 39 And when did we see you sick or in prison and visit you?' 40 And the King will answer them, 'Truly, I say to you, as you did it to one of the least of these my brothers, you did it to me.'

41 "Then he will say to those on his left, 'Depart from me, you cursed, into the eternal fire prepared for the devil and his angels. 42 For I was hungry and you gave me no food, I was thirsty and you gave me no drink, 43 I was a stranger and you did not welcome me, naked and you did not clothe me, sick and in prison and you did not visit me.'

44 Then they also will answer, saying, 'Lord, when did we see you hungry or thirsty or a stranger or naked or sick or in prison, and did not minister to you?' 45 Then he will answer them, saying, 'Truly, I say to you, as you did not do it to one of the least of these, you did not do it to me.' 46 And these will go away into eternal punishment, but the righteous into eternal life (Matthew 25:31-46).

lesson two quick notes

James, Jesus' brother, wrote the book of James around AD 45. The wisdom that James writes in his letter is a great summary highlighting what the actions of an everyday Christian should look like. Likewise, it gives a good tension to Paul's teachings that it is faith alone by which saves us. While that is absolute, James reminds us that, "...faith without action is dead" (James 2:26). We cannot only be content with receiving our faith and with our salvation, but we must always think about others. James outlines what it looks like being a Christian who is full of action and has their focus set on sharing the good news of Jesus with those around them and transforming their communities.

James 2:1-7

James reminds us that there is no difference between a rich or a poor man. We should not honor one over the other because God does not show partiality to one over the other. God has given the poor wealth in their deep faith and is heirs to the kingdom of God. God does not honor a rich man more than a poor man, neither should we.

James 2:8-13

James reminds us of the command that God gave to the Levites, "You shall not hate your brother in your heart..." (Leviticus 19:17). Jesus says to love your neighbor and makes this the second greatest commandment in the Bible in Mark 12:29. We must love our neighbors as ourselves because failing at this one commandment is like forgetting to obey any of the Bible. James then urges us to have mercy on our neighbors just as we are free from the law.

James 2:14-17

James brings us to the key point of this chapter that if you have vibrant faith, you must also have a heartfelt yearning to do good to others. There is a difference in faith that compels a person to help those that are in need, and the faith a person has that only cares about themselves. He gives the example that it does no good to tell someone that needs clothing and food to, "Go in peace, be warmed and filled" (James 2:16), and do nothing to help them have that warmth and food. He argues that the same worthlessness comes from someone who has faith but does nothing good with it.

James 2:18-26

James shares that you cannot separate faith and works. He says that faith cannot be separated from works, but that we show faith by our works. It is not merely a question of faith or works, but that if you have faith, your faith is outwardly shown by good works. James shows us in two quick examples of Abraham and Rahab good works should complete that faith.

Matthew 25:31-46

In this passage Jesus gets straightforward with the seriousness of how our actions affect us when He comes back. With all the nations gathered together, Jesus will separate those that inherit the kingdom of God from those who will not by the good deeds they did. Those that inherit the kingdom are those that feed the hungry, give water to the thirsty, are welcoming to strangers, clothe the naked, and visit the sick and imprisoned. Jesus explains that by caring for these that are less fortunate, you care for He Himself. Those that do not feed the hungry, give water to the thirsty, welcome strangers, clothe the naked, or visit the sick and imprisoned are cast into the eternal fire prepared for the devil and his angels.

lesson two group review & discussion

Go over last week's group homework from lesson one and talk about it.

Discussion

These two passages of the Bible show the seriousness of how we "walk out" our faith. While faith in Christ as our savior alone secures our salvation, we must always live out that faith by our actions. In a quick few verses, James and Jesus show how worthless faith is without action. Even though many times we perceive the rich to be important, James explains how the poor have the "deck" stacked in their favor. In many places, the Bible shows how the poor and those that are in need are important figures in God's overall plan and how much He cares about them. Likewise, the Bible also points out how the rich will have a harder time entering the Kingdom of God than anyone else (Matthew 19:24).

- According to these passages, how much does God care about the poor or does the reference to the poor have some other meaning?

- Go around the room and each person share whether they have had any ongoing experience helping the poor and what that was.

- According to these passages, how do you think the poor differ from the rich? Each person name a difference.

- How are faith and works linked according to James?

- Is your faith linked to works or are your works linked to faith? Each person describe how they feel their faith and works are linked.

- Do you think we have an obligation to get involved with taking care of the poor ourselves other than the association we have with their care through our church's involvement?

- Go around the room and each person share an idea of how your group can get involved ongoing with taking care of the poor.

lesson two next steps

When we read something in the Bible that is there to make our Christian walk better we should learn to jump at the opportunity to to apply it to our own lives. Work through the steps below to apply the truths in this lesson to your own life. You need not share this with the group; it is between you and God.

- Do you perceive yourself as rich, poor, or somewhere in the middle?

- Do you have a tendency to treat the wealthy better or more honorable than the poor?

- Do you really love your neighbors? Who should we consider a neighbor?

- Who is a neighbor or someone that you have a tough time loving?

- What steps are you going to take to love that person that is tough to love?

- Does your faith compel you to live that faith out by doing good deeds? If so how?

- If your faith is not linked to doing good works, what are the steps you are going to take this week to change that?

- If today were the day that Matthew 25:31-46 references, do you think you would be a sheep or a goat? Why? Where would your destination be according to that scripture?

- What steps can you take to care for those that are less fortunate?

Flip to Appendix and answer the Character-Building Questions.

lesson two prayer points

- Pray for the poor in your city that God would supply for them all they need.

- Pray for the rich in your city.

- Pray that God would show you a way as a group to start or get involved in an ongoing project that puts each of you in a position to help the poor and needy in your city.

Other Group Prayer Needs:

lesson two group homework

Finish this page for next week's study and bring your work with you to group.

- From the ideas you came up with as a group or on your own, list steps that you as an individual will take to get involved with helping the poor and in need this next month.

- Come up with a list of things that you could do and will commit to throughout this next year to take care of the poor and needy.

Memorize this passage:

> What good is it, my brothers, if someone says he has faith but does not have works? Can that faith save him? If a brother or sister is poorly clothed and lacking in daily food, and one of you says to them, "Go in peace, be warmed and filled," without giving them the things needed for the body, what good is that? So also faith by itself, if it does not have works, is dead (James 2:14-17).

Journal Pages

This is a great opportunity to journal what you are learning or the action steps you want to take based on this lesson. Doing so will keep all your notes and journaling in this book as future reference. Start by taking a few minutes to pray and ask Jesus to bring to light all you are learning and what transformational changes you can make in your life. If you are reading this in an electronic version, make a digital note and journal.

Journal Pages

III

EQUIPPED

THREE
EQUIPPED

Ephesians 4:1-32

Unity in the Body of Christ
1 I therefore, a prisoner for the Lord, urge you to walk in a manner worthy of the calling to which you have been called, 2 with all humility and gentleness, with patience, bearing with one another in love, 3 eager to maintain the unity of the Spirit in the bond of peace. 4 There is one body and one Spirit--just as you were called to the one hope that belongs to your call-- 5 one Lord, one faith, one baptism, 6 one God and Father of all, who is over all and through all and in all. 7 But grace was given to each one of us according to the measure of Christ's gift. 8 Therefore it says,

"When he ascended on high he led a host of captives,
and he gave gifts to men."

(In saying, 'He ascended,' what does it mean but that he had also descended into the lower regions, the earth? 10 He who descended is the one who also ascended far above all the heavens, that he might fill all things.) 11 And he gave the apostles, the prophets, the evangelists, the shepherds and teachers, 12 to equip the saints for the work of ministry, for building up the body of Christ, 13 until we all attain to the unity of the faith and of the knowledge of the Son of God, to mature manhood, to the measure of the stature of the fullness of Christ, 14 so that we may no longer be children, tossed to and fro by the waves and carried about by every wind of doctrine, by human cunning, by craftiness in deceitful schemes. 15 Rather, speaking the truth in love, we are to grow up in every way into him who is the head, into Christ, 16 from whom the whole body, joined and held together by every joint with which it is equipped, when each part is working properly, makes the body grow so that it builds itself up in love.

The New Life

17 Now this I say and testify in the Lord, that you must no longer walk as the Gentiles do, in the futility of their minds. 18 They are darkened in their understanding, alienated from the life of God because of the ignorance that is in them, due to their hardness of heart. 19 They have become callous and have given themselves up to sensuality, greedy to practice every kind of impurity. 20 But that is not the way you learned Christ!-- 21 assuming that you have heard about him and were taught in him, as the truth is in Jesus, 22 to put off your old self, which belongs to your former manner of life and is corrupt through deceitful desires, 23 and to be renewed in the spirit of your minds, 24 and to put on the new self, created after the likeness of God in true righteousness and holiness.

25 Therefore, having put away falsehood, let each one of you speak the truth with his neighbor, for we are members one of another. 26 Be angry and do not sin; do not let the sun go down on your anger, 27 and give no opportunity to the devil. 28 Let the thief no longer steal, but rather let him labor, doing honest work with his own hands, so that he may have something to share with anyone in need. 29 Let no corrupting talk come out of your mouths, but only such as is good for building up, as fits the occasion, that it may give grace to those who hear. 30 And do not grieve the Holy Spirit of God, by whom you were sealed for the day of redemption. 31 Let all bitterness and wrath and anger and clamor and slander be put away from you, along with all malice. 32 Be kind to one another, tenderhearted, forgiving one another, as God in Christ forgave you (Ephesians 4:1-32).

lesson three quick notes

Paul wrote the book of Ephesians to the churches of Ephesus on his third missionary journey around AD 60. Paul packed Ephesians with many gems just waiting for discovery by Christians. Like many of his other letters, Ephesians revisits who we are in Christ, our salvation secured by faith, and guidelines for Christian families. Ephesians 4 is a power-packed chapter reminding us more about Christian character and how we must be transformed in Christ.

Ephesians 4:1-8

Paul urges us to walk in a way that honors our heritage as Christians with humility, patience, love, unity, and peace. He reminds us there is only one body, spirit, one hope, one Lord, one faith, one baptism, one God who is over everything, and in everything. We are each given a certain measure of grace, which is a gift from Christ.

Ephesians 4:9-16

Paul reminds us that Jesus was here on the earth and also in heaven so He would fulfill all things. Jesus gave positions to some to be equippers. God gave these equippers or teachers who are apostles, prophets, evangelists, shepherds (pastors), and teachers to the church for a specific reason. We often refer to these positions as the "five-fold ministry." Their jobs are to equip the church to do the work of the ministry, for building up the body of Christ into mature Christians knowing the Bible and its doctrine, and stand firm in their faith. Each believer should be a "minister," trained up by the five-fold ministry. Many times we get this sideways, we think the believers go to church and the paid staff are the ones who do the ministry. The fact is, the church is more like a college and the equippers (five-fold ministry) are the professors. They are there to instruct and teach the believer how to be a firm believer and to be a unified church with the reputation of Christ Himself. Then the believers unified (the Church) with the likeness of Christ Himself, transform their community. One reason a professional pastor's job is so tough is because many times he is the only one who trains the new Christians, takes care of daily church administration, counsels members, preaches on Sunday where he is to make new converts from a one-hour message. Many have referred to churches as hospitals where the sick keep getting sicker and the doctor, the pastor, keeps administering the same diagnosis and treatment to the same people repeatedly. Instead, Paul urges us to grow up in every way into Christ. With the entire body, the Church, joined and equipped and working properly, it can make the body grow and make disciples (Matthew 28:19). As the Church, we need to grow up strong like Christ with the help of those Jesus gave us to learn from and do the ministry that many times we have grown to believe is the pastor's job. Pastors, apostles, prophets, evangelists, and teachers are those that Jesus gave to teach us to be strong Christians so we can go out and make disciples.

Ephesians 4:17-24

Paul encourages believers to walk as strong Christians and the contrasts the difference to the Gentiles who are steeped in sin. This comparison is still relevant today when looking at Christians and nonbelievers. A nonbeliever has a hard time understanding the gospel. "They are darkened in their understanding, alienated from the life of God because of the ignorance is in them..." (Ephesians 4:18). The nonbeliever has become insensitive and alienated from God because of their lack of understanding and hard hearts. Paul lists their practice of sensuality, greed, and every kind of impurity, then contrasts that with reminding the Ephesians and us we were not taught those things associated with the truth of Jesus. Instead, we are to abandon our old sinful ways and to allow the renewal of our minds while taking on a new self that is made in the likeness of God in true righteousness and holiness.

Paul reminds the Corinthians of their blindness toward God, along the same lines:

> In their case the god of this world has blinded the minds of the unbelievers, to keep them from seeing the light of the gospel of the glory of Christ, who is the image of God (2 Corinthians 4:4).

Even though the mind of the nonbeliever is blind they know that God exists and is the creator of the world as Paul states to the Romans,

> For his invisible attributes, namely, his eternal power and divine nature, have been clearly perceived, ever since the creation of the world, in the things that have been made. So they are without excuse (Romans 1:20).

Ephesians 4:25-32

Paul finishes Ephesians 4 by listing nine other ways the Christian is to differ from the nonbeliever. We are to be truthful with our neighbors. If we are angry, be angry, but not in a way that we sin and do not let the sun go down on our anger. Don't steal, but work for our wages. Do not speak in dishonoring ways, but only encouraging ways. Obey the Holy Spirit, do not be bitter or full of rage. Be kind to each other, forgiving one another as God forgave us.

lesson three group review & discussion

Go over last week's group homework from lesson one and talk about it.

Discussion

Chapter 4 of Ephesians gives us an even clearer insight into more character attributes we are to work towards as Christians. With our salvation secured by faith and our lives transformed by Christ, Paul introduces the "professors" Jesus gives that equip us so we can become strong Christians. Pastors, apostles, prophets, evangelists, and teachers are our professors given by Jesus to equip us to be the Church so we can do the work of the ministry. Paul then helps us to understand how we are to work together in unity as the Church to help the rest of the world become disciples of Jesus.

- Go around the room and each person share with the group a little about how you began going to church, your salvation experience (if one), and your present involvement in the church.

- Have you ever thought of the individual members of the Church as a body with a head, limbs, fingers, etc? How does this seem to make the workload of the church easier?

- What is the difference in the Church universal as the universal body of believers, and a church a person may attend weekly?

- Go around the room and discuss how viewing the apostle, prophet, evangelist, pastor, and teacher as "professors" given to educate us so we can do ministry differs from how you may have viewed them before.

- Do you think most Christians in the world have been content to let the apostle, prophet, evangelist, pastor, and teacher do most of the work, and see their part as going to church on Sundays?

- Go around the room and share the impact on the community and world if all the members of your church or even small group took an active role in taking on most of the responsibilities that paid church staff have.

- According to this chapter, do certain believers have more of a "call to ministry" than others? Are we all "called" to do the same work in making disciples and transforming our communities?

- Going around the room, discuss how viewing the church building as a college, and the pastors as professors, help you define your role as the one who is taught and then goes out to use that education in discipling the world.

- How can we as members of our church help reduce the load of responsibilities and duties of the Pastor's and staff so they can spend more time as teachers equipping other believers?

lesson three next steps

When we read something in the Bible that is there to make our Christian walk better we should learn to jump at the opportunity to to apply it to our own lives. Work through the steps below to apply the truths in this lesson to your own life. You need not share this with the group; it is between you and God.

- Do you live out your Christian life in a way that honors your role as a child of God?

- How are you regarding being Humble? Patient? Loving? Unified with other Christians? Peaceful?

- Do you feel God's grace in your life? If so, how does grace help you?

- Are you one who God calls to equip full-time (Apostle, Prophet, Evangelist, Pastor, or Teacher)? If so, what steps are you going to take to become educated to fill that role?

- On a scale of 1-10 (10 the most), how mature do you see yourself as a Christian? What steps can you take today that will help you grow one step closer to a 10?

- Now that you understand that every believer is to be doing ministry and making disciples, how can you seek to engage in your role?

- If the "five-fold" ministry is our professors designed to train and equip us, how can you take your role as a student and future graduate more serious? Could diligent note-taking in church, taking each message like a college lecture with an exam at the end, or even extra study of the text from Sundays help you learn the information better?

- Since the "five-fold" ministry is a gift for us from Christ, how should we be treating them differently than we do today, if any? Is it time to let them off the hook for doing all the work in the church and take our rightful place in the mix some place?

- Which of the Christian characteristics that Paul

lists from Ephesians 4: 17-32 do you need to work on more? List out the steps you plan to take to accomplish your goal.

Flip to Appendix and answer the Character-Building Questions.

lesson three prayer points

- Pray for the church as a unified body worldwide.

- Pray for those in your church that are apostles, prophets, evangelists, pastors, and teachers.

- Pray for each member of your small group that they would mature even more than they are now.

- Pray for each member of your small group that they would take seriously their role as a minister and that God would begin showing them how to make disciples.

Other Group Prayer Needs:

lesson three group homework

F inish this page for next week's study and bring your work with you to group.

- Pray and ask God what part of Christ's body you are. Wrestle with your gifts and what passions you have while making a list of where you can get involved in your local or home church. What would you be excellent at?

- Have you answered the "call" of ministry in your own life? We can see that from this study we are all "called" to ministry. Some have answered that call and others are getting around to it. Spend some time with your pastor or mentor if possible, but at least God and accept the call you have, and then write the steps you are going to take to make sure you get involved with the role in ministry you are called to. You may feel you are called to the "five-fold ministry".

- List how you can begin taking on responsibilities at your church and reduce the load of work for the pastors and staff. Set up an appointment this week with your pastor, mentor, or parent to explore the possibilities.

Memorize this passage:

> I therefore, a prisoner for the Lord, urge you to walk in a manner worthy of the calling to which you have been called, with all humility and gentleness, with patience, bearing with one another in love, eager to maintain the unity of the Spirit in the bond of peace (Ephesians 4:1-3).

Journal Pages

This is a great opportunity to journal what you are learning or the action steps you want to take based on this lesson. Doing so will keep all your notes and journaling in this book as future reference. Start by taking a few minutes to pray and ask Jesus to bring to light all you are learning and what transformational changes you can make in your life. If you are reading this in an electronic version, make a digital note and journal.

Journal Pages

IV

TRANSFORMING OUR COMMUNITIES

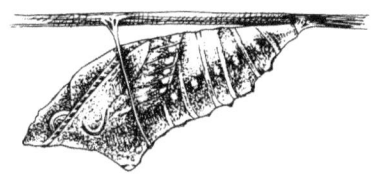

FOUR
TRANSFORMING OUR COMMUNITIES

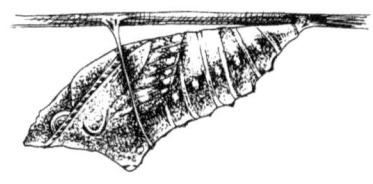

Acts 2:42-47 & Acts 4:32-35

The Fellowship of the Believers
42 And they devoted themselves to the apostles' teaching and the fellowship, to the breaking of bread and the prayers. 43 And awe came upon every soul, and many wonders and signs were being done through the apostles. 44 And all who believed were together and had all things in common. 45 And they were selling their possessions and belongings and distributing the proceeds to all, as any had need. 46 And day by day, attending the temple together and breaking bread in their homes, they received their food with glad and generous hearts, 47 praising God and having favor with all the people. And the Lord added to their number day by day those who were being saved (Acts 2:42-47).

They Had Everything in Common
32 Now the full number of those who believed were of one heart and soul, and no one said that any of the things

that belonged to him was his own, but they had everything in common. 33 And with great power the apostles were giving their testimony to the resurrection of the Lord Jesus, and great grace was upon them all. 34 There was not a needy person among them, for as many as were owners of lands or houses sold them and brought the proceeds of what was sold 35 and laid it at the apostles' feet, and it was distributed to each as any had need (Acts 4:32-35).

lesson four quick notes

The book of Acts is the story of the people who Jesus discipled Himself. Chronologically, Acts is the next book in the Bible just as Jesus ascends to heaven and leaves the disciples to do the work of making disciples that Jesus commissioned them to do. Acts is the book that shows us what the disciples did with the wealth of knowledge and teaching Jesus gave them. The book of Acts shows us exactly what Jesus expected those He discipled to put in place after He ascended to heaven. The New Testament Church under the original twelve gathered in house churches and generation after generation after them replicate that model. Like in last week's lesson, Jesus was the professor or teacher who equipped these disciples with all the knowledge, direction, and power so they could do the work of the ministry. Luke, one of Paul's disciples, wrote Acts around AD 62-64 and shows what it looks like when a small group of disciples takes Jesus' teachings seriously and sets out to change the world. How about your small group of disciples? Nothing is stopping you from making as big an impact as the early disciples. We have to remember, whether the church we attend has an emphasis on making disciples or not, Jesus commanded each believer to make disciples. It is not our church or its staff that will answer for our obedience when we stand before God. Each of us will stand on our own obedience to God's commands.

Acts 2:2-47

In last week's lesson we learned that the five-fold ministry is the professors who equip the believers, and these equipped believers devote themselves to the apostles' teaching. Then they also devoted themselves to fellowship, eating, and praying together. There is nothing complicated or expensive about families and friends eating and studying together! Luke tells us that awe came upon every soul, most likely both those in the small group and others they encountered daily. These believers cared for and loved each other in such a way that everything they had, they shared; they made sure that no one had any want or need. They were joyful, generous, and influenced everyone to be like them. Because of all this, they were well-liked and had significant influence. It cost the disciples everything, but their reward was God adding more believers to their revolution every day! Who would not want to be a part of a group of people like that?

Acts 4:32-35

The account by Luke in chapter 2 gives very much the same picture of this group of people changing the world. It does not seem a coincidence that Luke writes about it twice. The excitement was so electric he could not keep from trying to explain it again. Luke explains their unity as a group of believers where no one saw that anything they had was their own. They were laser-focused on telling about their time with Jesus and of His resurrection from the dead they had witnessed. No one was needy because those that had land and houses sold them and brought all the proceeds from the sales to the apostles to distribute to anyone who would have been otherwise in need. We have to remember these people were very much like your small group, these were not old lifelong friends that they had known all their lives. Some had known each other for longer than others, but their group of believers was growing at a rapid rate.

They started out as a group of men and families that Jesus

put together, some like Matthew the tax collector who began as enemies. Through grace and the commonality they had in Jesus, they worked at becoming a family.

In the church of Acts, all who BELIEVED were together and had all things in common, attending the temple together, breaking bread in their homes, receiving their food with glad and generous hearts. Then why were they attending the temple together? Did not Jesus do away with the temple customs?

Besides a place to worship, the Temple was where Jewish people met, exchanged news, and a part of their culture. Throughout my life these verses have been repeated as evidence that believers should gather at a church building. But the believers were gathering daily, eating together, and the Apostles were teaching them. They gathered to encourage and stir up each other to good works (Hebrews 10:24-25). The apostles were teaching the BELIEVERS all that Jesus had taught, so there was no need to go to the temple for teaching. "And they devoted themselves to the apostles' teaching and the fellowship, to the breaking of bread and the prayers" (Acts 2:42), so it was not for teaching. "Now Peter and John were going up to the temple at the hour of prayer, the ninth hour" (Acts 3:1). They heal a lame beggar, and he enters the temple with them, and Peter teaches the people and proclaimed Jesus resurrecting from the dead. (Acts 3:11-26 & Acts 4:2). Acts 4:33 says, "And with great power the apostles were giving their testimony to the resurrection of the Lord Jesus, and great grace was upon them all." The accounts are straightforward that they were going to the temple to evangelize and give their testimonies and to hear Peter's teaching, not to get their once-a-week sermon and sing a few praise and worship songs.

lesson four group review & discussion

Go over last week's group homework from lesson three and talk about it.

Discussion

These two groups of verses give us an incredible picture of what the early church looked like. Jesus had just been with them and ascended to heaven, leaving them the work of telling the rest of the world about Him. They did not differ from current day believers and had considerably fewer resources than we do today available to them to reach the entire world with the message of Jesus. Yet, they started in Jerusalem with what they had, and today we know the gospel message because of them. Their story of unselfish sharing and taking care of each other is unequaled. We must remember, it started with a small group of believers, very much like the group or family you are sitting in right now. The early disciples had nothing more than you. The miraculous had happened and now with Jesus' teachings and God's grace they decided once and for all to obey Jesus, love each other, and take the responsibility to tell the world about Jesus as He asked.

- Do most people in developed countries (USA, Europe, etc) have more possessions and belongings than they need?

- Go around the room and share how someone's generosity touched you in a deep way.

- Do you think the believers in Acts had a "stacked

deck" compared to us today so it would make it much easier for them to consider nothing their own but have everything in common?

- Go around the room and each person share why they think it was possible for the early believers in Acts to share everything and yet it is hard for us today to do the same.

- What makes the members in your small group or family any different (advantages or disadvantages) for it to be possible for your small group or family to duplicate the early believers in their model?

- What do you think it would take for your small group to begin and have a story like the group of believers here in Acts?

- Go around the room and share one material possession you do not need and will give to the group or church to be redistributed or sold to help someone else? What excess possessions do you own that the proceeds could help those in need?

- What steps can you take to always think about others' needs before purchasing excess possessions for yourself? Can we simplify our lives and use the excess God gives us to help others?

- Who might be on the other side of the world waiting to hear about Jesus that your small group might be the ones God has chosen to tell them? If your small group or family used the model explained here in Acts, how could you instantly impact your community? Church? World?

- Go around the room and each person answer the question: Can we as a small group or family make a commitment starting today to look more and more each week like the early church example? Can we make a commitment to each other to live, play, and do things together on an ongoing basis?

Living like the example of the early church takes a considerable commitment to each other. You will need to decide first that you love each other and will put aside your differences and begin living like the example of the church in Acts. You need not abandon your friends not in your small group, but you need to spend considerable time throughout the week with those in your small group or family. Think of them as your extended family, where they are always welcome to be around.

lesson four next steps

When we read something in the Bible that is there to make our Christian walk better we should learn to jump at the opportunity to to apply it to our own lives. Work through the steps below to apply the truths in this lesson to your own life. You need not share this with the group; it is between you and God.

- Are people awed by your example of Christ?

- Do you believe that God included these two groups of verses in the Bible as an example for us to follow or just a great story? Why or why not?

- If your small group or family took this example of the early church seriously, would you engage the process and give your heart and possessions to the effort?

- Would you be willing to engage the example of the early church even if your small group or church decided against such a model? Why or why not?

- Do you see all your possessions as God's to do with what He sees fit or do you see them as yours alone?

- Write some steps you will take this week to figure out what of yours you really need and what is excess. Once written will you make a commitment to live within your need and use the excess to help others that have a need?

- Come up with a plan for your finances to spend only what you need to live a life that looks like the outlined here in Acts 2 and 4. Include in your plan how you will use the excess to help those in your small group, church, or city on an ongoing basis.

- The question is not if we can live with less; it is instead are we willing to live with less and help others with what they need. Over half the world's population lives on $2 or less per day; if you tried, could you help a few of the less fortunate with a few bucks?

Flip to Appendix and answer the Character-Building Questions.

lesson four prayer points

- Pray for those that are in need all over the world. Over half the world's population live on $2 per day.

- Pray for God to show you and your group how you can live more like the example given in Acts of the early church.

- Pray that God will use your generosity and unity as believers to show the world that God sent Jesus.

- Pray for anyone in your small group that has a financial or resource need.

Other Group Prayer Needs:

lesson four group homework

There are those that attend your church and those in your community that has ongoing needs. Your church may have a community fund or ongoing community outreach that focuses on the needy in your community that your small group can be a part of. Chances are, there are more needs in your community than your church is meeting. Regardless, we can see by the example of the early church, it is our responsibility, not our church's to take care of each other and our community. Your small group can create an ongoing outreach that focuses on transforming your community, just like the example of the early church. By completing the two activities below your small group can begin and stay involved in transforming your city in a very real and tangible way. The goal would be to write a paragraph like the two we studied in Acts but in present-day tense about your small group.

Holiday Activity

Get out your calendars and figure out when the next holiday is coming up. (Thanksgiving, Christmas, Easter, etc.) Come up with a grocery list, including gifts, of things that you could take to a family in your community that has a need. Have each person or family in your group sign up to bring several items to the next group or if the holiday is only days away get them together quicker. Wrap the gifts and prepare the food if needed. As a small group, take the carload of stuff to the family and if possible stay and visit with them. Write up the activity in a paragraph and give it to your church staff, explaining to them what you did. If the people you are helping are comfortable, take pictures and start a small group scrapbook of your activity and future ones to come.

In addition, schedule to do one of the following as a group:

- Visit a homeless shelter and help prepare and serve the meal.

- Visit a local school and clean up their school grounds.

- Buy a loaf of bread, a jar of peanut butter and one of jelly and go to a poor area of town and make peanut butter and jelly sandwiches and pass them out to the homeless.

- Walk your downtown area and pray for the government.

- Volunteer as a group at one of your church's outreaches to the less fortunate. If your church does not have an outreach like this organize one.

Memorize this passage:

> Now the full number of those who believed were of one heart and soul, and no one said that any of the things that belonged to him was his own, but they had everything in common. And with great power the apostles were giving their testimony to the resurrection of the Lord Jesus, and great grace was upon them all (Acts 4:32 & 33).

Journal Pages

This is a great opportunity to journal what you are learning or the action steps you want to take based on this lesson. Doing so will keep all your notes and journaling in this book as future reference. Start by taking a few minutes to pray and ask Jesus to bring to light all you are learning and what transformational changes you can make in your life. If you are reading this in an electronic version, make a digital note and journal.

Journal Pages

V

OUR JOB OF EVANGELISM

FIVE
OUR JOB OF EVANGELISM

John 4:1-42

Jesus and the Woman of Samaria

1 Now when Jesus learned that the Pharisees had heard that Jesus was making and baptizing more disciples than John 2 (although Jesus himself did not baptize, but only his disciples), 3 he left Judea and departed again for Galilee. 4 And he had to pass through Samaria. 5 So he came to a town of Samaria called Sychar, near the field that Jacob had given to his son Joseph. 6 Jacob's well was there; so Jesus, wearied as he was from his journey, was sitting beside the well. It was about the sixth hour.

7 A woman from Samaria came to draw water. Jesus said to her, "Give me a drink." 8 (For his disciples had gone away into the city to buy food.) 9 The Samaritan woman said to him, "How is it that you, a Jew, ask for a drink from me, a woman of Samaria?" (For Jews have no dealings with Samaritans.) 10 Jesus answered her, "If you knew the gift of

God, and who it is that is saying to you, 'Give me a drink,' you would have asked him, and he would have given you living water." 11 The woman than said to him, "Sir, you have nothing to draw water with, and the well is deep. Where do you get that living water? 12 Are you greater than our father Jacob? He gave us the well and drank from it himself, as did his sons and his livestock." 13 Jesus said to her, "Everyone who drinks of this water will be thirsty again, 14 but whoever drinks of the water that I will give him will never be thirsty again. The water that I will give him will become in him a spring of water welling up to eternal life." 15 The woman said to him, "Sir, give me this water, so that I will not be thirsty or have to come here to draw water."

16 Jesus said to her, "Go, call your husband, and come here." 17 The woman answered him, "I have no husband." Jesus said to her, "You are right in saying, 'I have no husband'; 18 for you have had five husbands, and the one you now have is not your husband. What you have said is true." 19 The woman said to him, "Sir, I perceive that you are a prophet. 20 Our fathers worshiped on this mountain, but you say that in Jerusalem is the place where people ought to worship." 21 Jesus said to her, "Woman, believe me, the hour is coming when neither on this mountain nor in Jerusalem will you worship the Father. 22 You worship what you do not know; we worship what we know, for salvation is from the Jews. 23 But the hour is coming, and is now here, when the true worshipers will worship the Father in spirit and truth, for the Father is seeking such people to worship him. 24 God is spirit, and those who worship him must worship in spirit and truth." 25 The woman said to him, "I know that Messiah is coming (he who is called Christ). When he comes, he will tell us all things." 26 Jesus said to her, "I who speak to you am he."

27 Just then his disciples came back. They marveled that he was talking with a woman, but no one said, "What do you seek?" or, "Why are you talking with her?" 28 So the woman left her water jar and went away into town and said to the people, 29 "Come, see a man who told me all that I ever did. Can this be the Christ?" 30 They went out of the town and were coming to him.

31 Meanwhile the disciples were urging him, saying, "Rabbi, eat." 32 But he said to them, "I have food to eat that you do not know about." 33 So the disciples said to one another, "Has anyone brought him something to eat?" 34 Jesus said to them, "My food is to do the will of him who sent me and to accomplish his work. 35 Do you not say, 'There are yet four months, then comes the harvest'? Look, I tell you, lift up your eyes, and see that the fields are white for harvest. 36 Already the one who reaps is receiving wages and gathering fruit for eternal life, so that sower and reaper may rejoice together. 37 For here the saying holds true, 'One sows and another reaps.' 38 I sent you to reap that for which you did not labor. Others have labored, and you have entered into their labor."

39 Many Samaritans from that town believed in him because of the woman's testimony, "He told me all that I ever did." 40 So when the Samaritans came to him, they asked him to stay with them, and he stayed there two days. 41 And many more believed because of his word. 42 They said to the woman, "It is no longer because of what you said that we believe, for we have heard for ourselves, and we know that this is indeed the Savior of the world (John 4:1-42).

lesson five quick notes

You may not have thought of yourself as a missionary or a minister before starting Transform 5 weeks ago. In these five weeks, we have not only learned that we are all ministers and missionaries of the gospel, but also that it is our primary role. Everything we do in work and play we should do in such a way that the world will see and want to know Jesus through our example. When we hear the word missionary we many times think of the people who stand up on Sunday mornings and tell us about the far-off lands, they have dedicated their lives to and show pictures of the children and people they are making a difference to. You are no less a missionary than they are. The only difference might be they are more focused on their mission versus what you are. You can change that focus and intensity. While God has directed their focus on making disciples of people in another part of the world, we focus on making disciples of people around us. If believers worldwide would focus on making disciples of those they know, there would be no need for "foreign missionaries." As in the story of the woman at the well, she immediately knew that her mission and responsibility was to tell everyone in her town that she had met Jesus.

John 4:1-6

Like in the story of the good Samaritan (Luke 10:29-37), Samaritans and Jews did not associate with each other, because one was a Jew and the other a Gentile. The meeting of Jesus and the Samaritan woman might seem like a chance meeting, but Jesus knew that the town of Sychar needed to meet Him. Many times what might seem like a chance meeting. God setting us up to see a miracle. In John 9 Jesus and the disciples come upon a man who had been blind since birth. The disciples, as were the beliefs of that time, assumed he was blind by God because he or his parents had sinned. When they asked Jesus who had sinned Jesus answered, "It was not that this man sinned, or his parents, but that the works of God might be displayed in him" (John 9:3). The man had been born blind so that Jesus would come by that very day, heal his blindness, and the rest of the events of that day would happen.

John 4:7-15

A Samaritan woman came to draw water in the middle of the day because she would be less likely to meet up with others of the town. Most in a town drew water early in the morning or in the evening when it was cooler. Because of her lifestyle of promiscuity and immorality, she looked down upon. This woman came to draw physical water but Jesus offers her the gift that she never expected she was worthy of living water.

John 4:16-26

It is clear the woman knows some about the Old Testament writings, but Jesus reveals through her lifestyle that what she knows about the Law is only head knowledge. She is in adultery and divorced from five marriages; it may have only been Jesus Himself that could have convinced this woman that she could turn from her life of sin. In fact, from her sentence in verse twenty-seven, she may hope that she will meet the Messiah one day, and He can tell her how to get out of the awful lifestyle she is in. This very day, through what seems like a chance meeting when she was trying to avoid others, and out of the millions of people in the world, she meets face to face with Jesus. We may think the people we meet and talk to are by chance. However, it is more likely that these people need to meet Jesus and as we have learned; you are the only physical Jesus they are going to meet here on this earth. If Jesus had been content with getting His drink and letting the woman go on her way, what would have been the fate of the woman? How about the fate of the town?

John 4:27-30

How long is the training, equipping, and discipleship from the time you become a believer after meeting Jesus until you head out to tell the next person about Jesus? Though the religiously trained may try to convince us it takes years to lead others to Jesus, but for this woman, her training lasted minutes. The lady left immediately, left the water jug (the old water), and led the town to Jesus. She did not sit through a single sermon, or worry about her past life, but knew others needed to meet Jesus. She was an instant missionary in her own town. Our transformation in Christ should lead to us transforming our community for God.

John 4:31-38

We should be able to see ourselves in both the woman and Jesus. First, Jesus met every one of us in a very similar place. Though the woman's sins and the ugliness of her life are very easy to see, our sins looked equally bad to Jesus when He found us. We should also see ourselves in Jesus because, as we have learned, when He ascended to heaven, He left us in His place. Does it make you wonder if those who meet you run back to those they know, urging them to come to meet you so they can be introduced to Jesus? Starting in verse 31, we see that Jesus did not have a hard time prioritizing His work. Though tired and hungry, Jesus knew that the "harvest" of this town was at hand and there was no time to be worrying about His own physical needs. Likewise, there are "fields" all around us every day that are "white for harvest" (John 4:35) but like the disciples, we may not see them, because we are too busy in the routine of our lives.

John 4:39-42

Many of the town believed in Jesus that day because of a woman who met Jesus, and she immediately told everyone else. The woman did what anyone who has met Jesus should do, "tell everyone else". Reading this story brings to question where we have misplaced the excitement after meeting Jesus that keeps us from telling everyone we meet? There is no better time to tell everyone you know about Jesus than the second you meet Him for the first time.

lesson five group review & discussion

Go over last week's group homework from lesson four and talk about it.

Discussion

There is little difference in the woman that Jesus met at the well in Sychar and ourselves. We were both in a terrible state of life when we met Jesus, and we were only concerned about our physical needs when what we need is the living water that comes only from Jesus. Once we meet Jesus and accept Him as our Savior from sin, there is only one thing to do next, "go tell everyone else". When we look at the story from Jesus' side, we have a job left to fulfill and that is to focus on the harvest. In both cases the task is the same, tell everyone we meet about the Savior and introduce them to Him so they do not have to take our word for it, but they can see and experience His transformation for themselves.

- Go around the room and each person explain what state of life most people are in when they meet Jesus the first time.

- Was the woman meeting Jesus a meeting of chance or did Jesus know the woman would be there and what would happen when He met her?

- Does each person in your group think there were people in the town where the woman lived that would have missed the chance at meeting Jesus had the woman not went and told the town about Him? Samaritans were considered half-Gentile.

- Do you think the woman acted too fast in immediately believing she had the qualifications to tell others about Jesus and instead should have waited until she fully understood the gospel? How trained up should a person be before telling others about Jesus?

- Go around the room and each person give input on how comfortable they are with telling others about Jesus. What situations are you most comfortable and which very uncomfortable?

- Go around the room and each person name a family or individual in your neighborhood that you believe needs to meet Jesus? How do you know? What about a believer would be noticeable to you?

- Are we too busy in the routines of our daily lives to take time to focus on the people that God is placing in front of us daily so we can introduce them to Jesus?

- What can you do to be more like the woman who left her jar of water at the well so she could run into the town and tell everyone about Jesus?

lesson five next steps

When we read something in the Bible that is there to make our Christian walk better we should learn to jump at the opportunity to to apply it to our own lives. Work through the steps below to apply the truths in this lesson to your own life. You need not share this with the group; it is between you and God.

- The woman at the well had a secret life of sin that she thought she was going to keep from Jesus. Though Jesus knows all things, is there anything current in your life that you are ashamed to share with Jesus?

- Samaritans and Jews did not associate with each other, and by those standards alone Jesus was counter-cultural in talking to the Samaritan woman. Is there any circumstance that you would have a hard time being counter-cultural to tell the people about Jesus? If so, how can you overcome your differences?

- Think back. How many times in this last week did you have a chance meeting with people when actually they might have been placed there like the Samaritan woman so you could introduce them to Jesus? How many times this year?

- How long have you known Jesus? Now how long do you feel you have had the qualifications to introduce others to Jesus? If you do not feel qualified, then write five steps you can take this week to get the training you need to introduce others to Jesus.

- Is being uncomfortable about sharing Jesus a valid reason to avoid inviting others to meet and know Jesus? Write three steps you can take this week to be more comfortable inviting those Jesus places in your life to know Him.

- Who are two people that you believe need to meet Jesus? Write the steps you are going to take in the next week to get one step closer to introducing them to Jesus.

- Is your daily and weekly routine busy? If so, your friends and neighbors are most likely not the only ones suffering from you not modeling Jesus to them. Can you say that you spend as much time with your family as Jesus would if He were you in your family?

- The water jar the Samaritan woman left at the well could represent her embarrassment, her work, or her excuses. So she left her old life to share Jesus with those that did not even like her because of her chosen lifestyle. Are you willing to leave your work each day at an appropriate time to spend the rest of the evening with your family showing them Jesus? Is there embarrassment or excuses that you need to overcome to tell those you know about Jesus? How can you take steps to make that happen?

- Our families are as important as any other people on the earth that we should introduce to Jesus. The time you give your family is more important than anything else you could be doing. The family should come before anything, and the years you have children around the house are monumental that you are present. How many stories have you heard where it starts out "My Mother or Father were never at home..."? At what point will your spouse and children perceive that you were never around? Even as ministers of the gospel, "ministry" to our families comes first. What can you do to make sure you have quality time each week with your family?

Flip to Appendix and answer the Character-Building Questions.

lesson five prayer points

- Pray for each of your neighborhoods and city and all the people in them that need to meet Jesus.

- Pray for each member in your small group that in the coming weeks you each could figure out how to invite the people you encounter each week to meet Jesus.

- Pray that God would open up conversations with the people you encounter each week so that you have a clear opportunity to invite them to meet Jesus.

Other Group Prayer Needs:

lesson five group homework

F inish this page for next week's study and bring your work with you to group.

- The woman left her water jar and went away into town and said to the people, "Come, see a man who told me all that I ever did. Can this be the Christ?" They went out of the town and were coming to him" (John 4:28-30).

- Who lives in your neighborhood or next door, works with you, mows your grass, is your clerk at the grocery store, or is even a family member that you could invite to "Come meet Jesus"?

- It is time to get your focus honed to realize that your "town" is all around you and all you need to do is invite them to "Come meet Jesus", and He will do the rest. Make a list of everyone you encounter in a week that may need to meet Jesus.

- Some of those you listed you are closer to than others. Write their names again, then next to them write a brief description of how you could invite each of them to meet Jesus. If you are a homemaker or stay at home mom, you could have tea or lunch with each of the other women in your neighborhood. If you work, invite each co-worker to lunch throughout the next months.

- Can you start a small group that meets weekly specifically for your neighborhood? Can you meet with your family each week sharing Bible stories? The books listed in the back of this book are excellent resources to use with your small group or family.

Memorize this passage:

I therefore, a prisoner for the Lord, urge you to walk in a manner worthy of the calling to which you have been called, with all humility and gentleness, with patience, bearing with one another in love, eager to maintain the unity of the Spirit in the bond of peace (Ephesians 4:1-3).

Journal Pages

This is a great opportunity to journal what you are learning or the action steps you want to take based on this lesson. Doing so will keep all your notes and journaling in this book as future reference. Start by taking a few minutes to pray and ask Jesus to bring to light all you are learning and what transformational changes you can make in your life. If you are reading this in an electronic version, make a digital note and journal.

Journal Pages

VI

UNITY

SIX
UNITY

Colossians 3:12-17, John 17:20-26, 1 Peter 4:8-10,

Put On the New Self

12 Put on then, as God's chosen ones, holy and beloved, compassionate hearts, kindness, humility, meekness, and patience, 13 bearing with one another and, if one has
a complaint against another, forgiving each other; as the Lord has forgiven you, so you also must forgive. 14 And above all these put on love, which binds everything together
in perfect harmony. 15 And let the peace of Christ rule in your hearts, to which indeed you were called in one body. And be thankful. 16 Let the word of Christ dwell in you richly, teaching and admonishing one another in all wisdom, singing psalms and hymns and spiritual songs, with thankfulness in your hearts to God. 17 And whatever you do, in word or deed, do everything in the name of the Lord Jesus, giving thanks to God the Father through him (Colossians 3:12-17).

The High Priestly Prayer

20 "I do not ask for these only, but also for those who will believe in me through their word, 21 that they may all be one, just as you, Father, are in me, and I in you, that they also may be in us, so that the world may believe that you have sent me. 22 The glory that you have given me I have given to them, that they may be one even as we are one, 23 I in them and you in me, that they may become perfectly one, so that the world may know that you sent me and loved them even as you loved me. 24 Father, I desire that they also, whom you have given me, may be with me where I am, to see my glory that you have given me because you loved me before the foundation of the world. 25 O righteous Father, even though the world does not know you, I know you, and these know that you have sent me. 26 I made known to them your name, and I will continue to make it known, that the love with which you have loved me may be in them, and I in them" (John 17:20-26).

Stewards of God's Grace

8 Above all, keep loving one another earnestly, since love covers a multitude of sins. 9 Show hospitality to one another without grumbling. 10 As each has received a gift, use it to serve one another, as good stewards of God's varied grace: 11 whoever speaks, as one who speaks oracles of God; whoever serves, as one who serves by the strength that God supplies--in order that in everything God may be glorified through Jesus Christ. To him belong glory and dominion forever and ever. Amen (1 Peter 4:8-10).

I Am The True Vine

13 Greater love has no one than this, that someone lay down his life for his friends. 14 You are my friends if you do what I command you. 15 No longer do I call you servants,

for the servant does not know what his master is doing; but I have called you friends, for all that

I have heard from my Father I have made known to you. 16 You did not choose me, but I chose you and appointed you that you should go and bear fruit and that your fruit should abide, so that whatever you ask the Father in my name, he may give it to you. 17 These things I command you, so that you will love one another (John 15:13-17).

One Body with Many Members

12 For just as the body is one and has many members, and all the members of the body, though many, are one body, so it is with Christ. 13 For in one Spirit we were all baptized into one body-- Jews or Greeks, slaves or free--and all were made to drink of one Spirit.

14 For the body does not consist of one member but of many. 15 If the foot should say, "Because I am not a hand, I do not belong to the body," that would not make it any less a part of the body. 16 And if the ear should say, "Because I am not an eye, I do not belong to the body," that would not make it any less a part of the body. 17 If the whole body were an eye, where would be the sense of hearing? If the whole body were an ear, where would be the sense of smell? 18 But as it is, God arranged the members in the body, each one of them, as he chose. 19 If all were a single member, where would the body be? 20 As it is, there are many parts, yet one body.

21 The eye cannot say to the hand, "I have no need of you," nor again the head to the feet, "I have no need of you." 22 On the contrary, the parts of the body that seem to be weaker are indispensable, 23 and on those parts of the body that we think less honorable we bestow the greater honor, and our unpresentable parts are treated with greater modesty, 24 which our more presentable parts do not require. But God has so composed the body, giving greater

honor to the part that lacked it, 25 that there may be no division in the body, but that the members may have the same care for one another. 26 If one member suffers, all suffer together; if one member is honored, all rejoice together (1 Corinthians 12:12-26).

The Great Commandment

34 But when the Pharisees heard that he had silenced the Sadducees, they gathered together. 35 And one of them, a lawyer, asked him a question to test him. 36 "Teacher, which is the great commandment in the Law?" 37 And he said to him, "You shall love the Lord your God with all your heart and with all your soul and with all your mind. 38 This is the great and first commandment. 39 And a second is like it: You shall love your neighbor as yourself. 40 On these two commandments depend all the Law and the Prophets" (Matthew 22:34-40).

lesson six quick notes

The Bible is a book of the most important letters ever written. Men, inspired by the Holy Spirit, wrote the words from the Creator of the universe to His children, who He loves more than anything else. It was so important that these letters get our attention that God put an exclamation point amongst them by sending His only Son to die for us. His son, Jesus, was God's ultimate gift to us, a love letter in human form. Jesus died a death on the cross, both because He loved the Father, being obedient to Him even unto death. The Bible is a love letter, full of tragedy, steeped with hope, and concluded with a promise that we as God's children will be with Him forever. The Bible is also a letter of instruction to us from our Father outlining how we should respond to His love for us. His instruction is for us to love each other and everyone else in the world just as He loves them. Our lesson this week centers on our unity as believers and keeping the second most important commandment in the Bible, "Love your neighbor as yourself" (Mark 12:31).

Colossians 1:12-17

Paul wrote Colossians to the church in Colossae around AD 60. The situation was a little like it had been in Galatia a few years earlier when Paul wrote Galatians. However, in Colossae, some teachers in the city were teaching untruths and were attempting to make the Christians adhere to unnecessary rules about meals and religious festivals. In Colossians 3:12-17, Paul addresses the importance of forgiving each other and the believers living in perfect harmony. Because we are one body, we should be peaceful, thankful, and encouraging to one another. We should worship, learn together and do everything in the name of Jesus, giving thanks to God through Him.

John 17:20

The last words of a man condemned to death and about to go through the worse beating and hanging is history, are some of His most important. As Jesus was talking to His Father in the garden just before he was arrested and crucified, He was thinking about us more than He was thinking about Himself. He prayed to the Father that we would have unity as one as He Himself and His Father are one. The Trinity of God, the Son, and the Holy Spirit are inseparable. Jesus repeats twice His desire that we would be one so that the world would believe that the Father sent Him. This is perhaps the most profound statement about evangelism in the Bible. Jesus says that if we are perfectly one just like the Trinity is one, that the world will know that God sent Jesus and that the Father loves them. More than any other way that Jesus gave us to carry on His work here on earth is to love each other and be perfectly one.

1 Peter 4:8-10

Peter penned these verses somewhere around AD 62-64 and wrote them to Jewish Christians who were being tortured, killed, and driven out of Jerusalem by the Roman Empire. These Christians knew suffering as did Peter who would be killed just years after writing this book. Understanding some of the most extreme conditions in which to love someone, Peter encourages these Christians to continue loving each other. He urges them to be friendly to each other and to even strangers without complaining. He continues to encourage them to use their gifts given by God to help each other because to do this is just as God is doing it Himself and it glorifies Him.

John 15:13-17

Yet another time in the gospels Jesus gives us an extreme example of what it means to love by being willing to give our own lives for others. Jesus calls us His friend and tells us He has told us everything that God has told Him. Jesus made the first move by choosing us and as the correct response to Him choosing and appointing us, we should bear fruit (make true disciples) so that whatever you ask our Father in His name, he may give it to you.

> You did not choose me, but I chose you and appointed you that you should go and bear fruit and that your fruit should abide, so that whatever you ask the Father in my name, he may give it to you. (John 15:16)

The condition for this promise, of God giving us what we ask, is that we make disciples that abide in Jesus. Then if we keep Jesus' commandments which enables us to abide in Jesus' love, He promises His joy will be in us, and that our joy will be full.

> If you keep my commandments, you will abide in my love, just as I have kept my Father's commandments and abide in his love. These things I have spoken to you, that my joy may be in you, and that your joy may be full (John 15:10-11).

There is nothing other than eternity itself that I could wish more for than Jesus' joy overflowing in my life. That is such an incredible statement that Jesus will give us His joy to overflowing.

1 Corinthians 12:12-26

Paul wrote Corinthians during his third missionary trip to the church he had planted in the city of Corinth in Acts 18. The church in Corinth was having serious problems with moral issues that they were being influenced by daily. Issues about sexual immorality, lawsuits against each other, food offered to idols, and idolatry were causing divisions in the church. In the wicked city of Corinth, the temptations were becoming too much. Paul addresses all these issues in the first book of Corinthians. Here Paul illustrates how we as Christians are one body and being so we can be one and live in harmony. Paul explains that not only are we different parts of one body, but we were all baptized into Christ's body. We must remember and practice such unity and honor and take care of all the members of the body.

Matthew 22:34-40

Once again Jesus talks about how important it is for us to love each other and live in unity. Yet, this time He emphasizes how vital this is by showing us it is the second greatest commandment in the Bible. First, we must love God with all our heart, soul, and mind. Then we must love each other as we love ourselves. Whether or not you think you love yourself, you do. There may be things you dislike about yourself or your circumstances, but most of us make sure we fill our stomachs, get rest, seek pleasure, and even try to rid ourselves of pain. You take enough care of yourself to continue through each day fine. We should care about our neighbors as much.

lesson six group review & discussion

G o over last week's group homework from lesson five and talk about it.

Discussion

This grouping of verses throughout the New Testament gives us a glimpse of how important as believers, our love for each other, and unity is. There is no mistaking that God is serious about us loving each other. God, who has no sin, gave His only Son to redeem us from sin so we could have a relationship with Him. He then adopted us into His family and considers us His children. Since God has that much love for us, is it possible for us to look pass our differences and love each other? Loving one another does not require us to sacrifice our children like it did God.

- Does the word "love" get confusing because in the English language we use it for so many meanings? How many meanings of the word love can you come up with as a group?

- Is it easy to determine what the meaning of the word love is for each of these verses?

- Each person in the group give your opinion on whether you think most Christians love everyone else in the world. Do they love others with the degree of love that God has for everyone?

- Do you think most Christians exhibit the depth of

love in which each of these verses instructs us towards Non-Christians?

- Go around the room and each person give an example of how you in your own life could better love those around you, especially those in your small group.

- Go around the room and each name one person who is a Non-Christian that you could do a better job of loving as Christ loves you. Explain how you could show them God's love.

- Who is one person who is a Christian that you could work at being more unified with?

- If the body of Christ is many parts yet one body, what body part does each person in your small group think they are?

lesson six next steps

When we read something in the Bible that is there to make our Christian walk better we should learn to jump at the opportunity to to apply it to our own lives. Work through the steps below to apply the truths in this lesson to your own life. You need not share this with the group; it is between you and God.

- Explain the depth of love God has for you that He would send His only Son to die so He could repair the relationship with you destroyed by sin?

- Would most people that you know you say that you deeply love both Christians and Non- Christians? Why or why not?

- Who was the person you named in your group that was a Non-Christian that you could do a better job of loving as Christ loves you? Write three things that you could do this week to show them Christ's love.

- Who is a Christian that you could do a better job of showing Christ's love to? Write three things that you could do this week to show them Christ's love.

- Based on your spiritual gifts, what part of the body of Christ are you and do you try to do other body part's jobs? Do you do your own body part function well?

- How could you allow others to do their part as the body by sticking to your function and allowing them to do theirs?

- How could you show each member of your small group Christ's love more? List out each of their names and one thing you could do to show them Christ's love.

Flip to Appendix and answer the Character-Building Questions.

lesson six prayer points

- Pray for the unity of your small group and your church.

- Pray John 17: 21-26 together. "God, we pray that we may all be one, as you, Father, are in Christ, and Christ in you, that we also may be in them, so that the world may believe that you sent Christ. The glory that you have given Him he has given to us, that we may be one even as Christ and you are one, Christ in us and you in Him, that we may become perfectly one, so that the world may know that you sent Christ and loved them even as you loved Christ. Father, Christ desired that we are with Him where He is, to see His glory that you have given Him because you loved Him before the foundation of the world. O righteous Father, even though the world does not know you, Christ knows you, and we know that you have sent Him. Christ made known to us your name, and He continues to make it known, that the love with which you have loved Him may be in us, and Christ in us" (John 17: 21-26).

- Pray that those in your small group can show those

that do not know Christ love as He loves them with.

O ther Group Prayer Needs:

lesson six group homework

Since your last group activity and research, have you discovered how your small group can transform your community? Have you found a Non-Christian family in need? If not, your mission starts off this week with finding one. If you can get back in touch with the family that you served in Lesson 4, they are the family you want to use for this activity.

Once you have found the family or gotten back in touch with the family you used in Lesson 4, make an appointment with them for your group to come over for 45 minutes and visit with them. Find a time your entire group can do this and make the day and time convenient for the family, not your small group.

Before the visit:

- Find out if they drink coffee, tea, or something else and if there is anything they don't like or are allergic to.
- Go to your local grocery store and buy a dessert (carrot cake, lemon bundt cake, etc) that is not ordinary and a little more classy.
- Bring the fixings for hot tea, brewed coffee, or "tea party" types of drinks already fixed.
- Take plastic (fancy if you can find them) plates, utensils, and paper napkins, and a trash bag.
- Bring a notepad and pen.
- Try to bring small inexpensive gift.

NOTE: If it is around a holiday this is your chance to shine by blowing them away once more with groceries, gifts, toys for the kids, etc, etc.

On the visit:

- Let them know that you wanted to bring a little something (the drinks and dessert) to share with them and let them know they are special to you.
- Prepare all the food and drinks.
- The first 15 minutes of this time is about them, share about those in your group and very light-hearted stuff that shows them you care.
- The next 30 minutes ask them in a caring way what your group could do ongoing to help them and really make a difference. Let them know your group is there to make a difference and a commitment over the next several months. If they have no idea, then give them some ideas that you could do to help. Take notes!
- Let them know you are going to discuss it as a group and determine how many of the items you could meet as a group. Thank them for the visit, pray with them if possible.
- Before you leave clean up all the plates, utensils, napkins, and anything else that you used. The stuff you brought goes in the trash bag you brought and out the door with you.

Back at your next group:

- Determine how many of the needs you can meet as a group.
- Make a plan.
- Everyone commit to meet the needs and equally divide the tasks.
- Get back in touch with the family as soon as

possible after your group meets and let them know what you're going to do, and the time commitment you can make.

IMPORTANT

Your 6-week study is over, but this is a perfect opportunity to figure out as a group how often you can do a group activity like this. You can continue helping the same family until they are no longer in need or pick a new family each time. Doing two things with one family shows them you mean it, especially if you can engage in their problem and help them fix it.

- Can your small group do a project like this each month? Every two months?
- Make sure you do something like this in your small group for every major holiday, especially Thanksgiving and Christmas.
- Your small group could be on its way to a story like how the twelve disciples transformed their community- there is nothing stopping you.

Research what outreaches your church has coming up that everyone in your small group can volunteer to be a part of. In addition, find or create an outreach that your small group can commit to being a part of every eight weeks or more. Here is a question that you can discuss in your small group to make this commitment.

- Does everyone in your small group agree that it is important to involve yourselves ongoing in helping those in your community that have needs?
- What is an ongoing activity that the group can do at least every 8 weeks?

- How can we delegate the responsibilities and costs, if any?
- Plan the next activity and organize it before leaving this page.

Memorize this passage:

> And he said to him, "You shall love the Lord your God with all your heart and with all your soul and with all your mind. This is the great and first commandment. 39 And a second is like it: You shall love your neighbor as yourself. On these two commandments depend all the Law and the Prophets (Matthew 22:37-40).

Journal Pages

This is a great opportunity to journal what you are learning or the action steps you want to take based on this lesson. Doing so will keep all your notes and journaling in this book as future reference. Start by taking a few minutes to pray and ask Jesus to bring to light all you are learning and what transformational changes you can make in your life. If you are reading this in an electronic version, make a digital note and journal.

Journal Pages

APPENDIX

Character Building Questions

The best way to use these questions is to pick the same-gender partner to be accountable to each week. By asking each other these questions you can stay accountable to each other in your Christian walk and develop an exemplary Christian character.

1. Have you been a good example this week to of your transformation in Jesus Christ with both your words and actions?
2. Have you been involved in any way with sexually alluring material or allowed your mind to entertain inappropriate sexual thoughts about another this week?
3. Have you lacked integrity in your financial dealings or coveted something that does not belong to you?
4. Have you been honoring, understanding, and generous in your important relationships this week?
5. Have you damaged another person by your words, either behind their back or face-to-face?
6. Have you given in to an addictive behavior this past week? Explain.
7. Have you remained angry toward another?
8. Have you secretly wished for another's misfortune so you might excel?
9. Did you finish your Bible reading for group this week and hear from God? What are you going to do about it?
10. Have you been completely honest with yourself and your accountability partner?

ACCEPTING JESUS

There is a first time that each of us first encounter Jesus. You might have met Jesus many years ago, or it is possible you met Him and did not even realize it was Him. Half the world dies without ever knowing about Jesus. Along many people's everyday journey through life, they meet Jesus for the first time. It might be through a good deed, a book, a friend, or even a crisis. When the original twelve disciples met Jesus, they were working their daily jobs as fishermen. Once you meet Jesus, you must either accept or reject Him, as there is no middle ground on which to stand. For some, it takes their entire life to follow Him and for others only the time it takes to speak His name.

The first disciples were Jews and taught from a young age of the coming Christ, the Messiah. Even waiting years for Jesus to come it took many, time to accept that Jesus was in person amongst them. The first disciples met Jesus on an ordinary day. He walked up to them and asked them to follow Him. To be a disciple, you must first accept to follow Jesus as the Messiah.

A good place to learn more about Jesus and the good news He brought into the world is to start with the book of John in the Bible. Those who have accepted Jesus may have never committed to learning more of Him than what others have told them. The book of John is a great introduction to Jesus and His life.

Listen to your heart as you read; what is it saying to you? Ask Jesus to show you He is the Son of God and make that real to you. If you want to meet Jesus and settle it in your heart once-and-for-always, He will show you He is the Christ. Remember, He made you, knows you, and has been pursuing you since the day of your birth. He's been pursuing each of us since the day He created Adam and Eve in the garden.

Jesus, the Son of God died for your sins, rose from death on the third day, and will forgive you of your sins. The Bible says to be saved, a person must, "...repent and be baptized for the forgiveness of your sins" (Acts 2:38). Then you must put your trust in Jesus Christ and believe in Him, and you will be saved (Acts 16:31).

If you're ready to give your life to Jesus, start by repenting for your sins. Tell Him you are sorry for your sins and thank Him for giving His life on the cross for you. Tell Him you believe He rose to life on the third day, and He has saved you from your sins and death and that He has given you eternal life. Repent of your sins and begin trusting in Jesus and your salvation from eternity in Hell is secure. Find another Christian who can baptize you whether it be in the ocean, pool, or church.

It is that simple to accept Jesus, acknowledge that He is the creator of the universe and you, and start living your life with purpose. It is by faith that we believe in Jesus, and through that faith we are born again. Now, as we read in 1 Peter, we are "born again to a living hope through the resurrection of Jesus Christ from the dead, to an inheritance that is imperishable, undefiled, and unfading, kept in heaven for you, who by God's power are being guarded through faith for a salvation ready to be revealed in the last time" (1 Peter 1:3-5 ESV). Nothing and no one can take that gift of eternal life away from you. It doesn't mean your life gets easier; many of the disciples found there were more challenges to life. Jesus will transform your life like the disciples, giving it purpose, and use you to tell others of Him.

Once you accept Jesus, there is only one thing left to do, follow Him, and make disciples.

Taken from *Ancient Paths, Untangling the Complexity of Discipleship*, Scott Michael Ringo

EPILOGUE

Reminder

I write this as a reminder to myself more than anything. It is hard to remember what success in the Kingdom of God looks like. Doing the work of a disciple of Jesus' is hard work. Caring for and showing the love of Jesus to the surrounding community is a lifelong pursuit. It is easy to see why Jesus chose twelve disciples to help distribute the responsibilities. Doing this work daily by yourself will leave you wore out. Doing the work within a community of believers is fun and exciting. Jesus knew exactly what to model with His disciples to train them to carry on the work in a sustainable model. It is almost as easy to apprentice eight disciples as it is to disciple one. The challenge is to find believers that want to be true disciples and commit their time, energy, resources, and daily life to making disciples. Being a disciple of Jesus' is not going to a church building once a week to listen to a sermon, sing some songs, then waiting a year to mention Jesus to your neighbor through fellowship evangelism.

"Immediately they left their nets and followed Him" (Matthew 4:20). The disciples who followed Jesus immediately left everything the minute they met Jesus. Then they followed Him as a community of vagabonds learning to make disciples. This ragtag group of disciples of Jesus changed the world.

The process to get started may seem overwhelming, especially if you are looking for others to do this with. It is hard to find people who believe in Jesus, who want to follow Him in making disciples. Even if you are part of a small group from your church, you know how hard it is to get everyone to show up weekly. It is near impossible to have participation in ongoing activities to transform the surrounding community. As easy as it sounds, getting twelve or fewer people together once a week to eat, study, and care for each other is daunting.

Instead, if you are married, start with your spouse. If you have children, it is important to include them. If you are single, start with yourself and find someone of the same gender. If you have extended family in the same area of town include them. It is hard to have community or ongoing activity if your group is fifteen minutes away from each other. Begin studying the Bible and eating together once a week. If you are a family, commit to studying the Bible, eating most of your meals together, and helping those with need. Commit to an outreach activity like outlined in this book. If you are a family or close group of friends, it is easier to get rock solid commitment. If those in the group cannot commit from now on to getting together to study the Bible, eat together, and do outreach activities you need to find those that will. It will never work perfectly, but discipleship is about teaching others to be like Jesus as you become like Jesus. The twelve disciples wanted to follow Jesus and learn His ways. Jesus kept them engaged, learning, and in community with each other.

Stay Simple

The encouragement here is to start with whom you have, but make sure you build community with believers who have repented of their sins, trust Jesus and want to do the work of making disciples, not just carry a title. Stay small until you find or make committed disciples. Stay small even after you find committed disciples. There is nothing, if not less, to gain with a large group. Read and follow the Bible and the examples of Jesus, it needs no professional education. Success as a disciple of Jesus is in making other disciples who make disciples. Jesus says, "By this my Father is glorified, that you bear much fruit and so prove to be my disciples" (John 15:8). That verse is the definition of success in the Kingdom of God.

The group you are a part of may never be large, but there are few stories of size in the Bible. The Bible is one large story of God made up of all the smaller stories of obedient sons and daughters. To make a disciple proves you are a disciple of Jesus, and that is all that matters.

NOTES

Introduction

1. "Transform." Cambridge Dictionary. Accessed August 17, 2018. https://dictionary.cambridge.org/us/dictionary/english/transform.
2. Unless otherwise noted, all biblical passages referenced are in the English Standard Version.

ABOUT THE AUTHOR

Scott Michael Ringo is a seasoned author who writes from his experience around the world. Scott has had the fortune in life to be as the ancient explorers, living life at its fullest and always curiously looking down the unexplored, overgrown trails that lead to new beauty. Jumping aboard a schooner bound for the open sea or charting an island that needs finding, full of riches in every turn. Join with Scott and explore and discover this amazing world that God created for us to live our life glorifying Him by making disciples, while being in an intimate relationship with our passionate lover, Jesus.

Become a world-changer

What if we could sit around the campfire with Jesus and hear what He taught the disciples? Would we become world-changers like them?

A powerful Bible study through the book of James diving deep into the character traits that will make us a true disciple of Jesus.

Available at amazon.com/author/scottringo in print or ebook.

TITLES BY SCOTT MICHAEL RINGO

Ancient Paths, Untangling the Complexity of Discipleship

Coffee For One, Daily Devotions that Inspire

James, Lesson from a Fisher of Men

Simple Fundraising, Easy Non-Profit Fundraising

Explosive Marketing

Simple Non-Profit Fundraising

www.ingramcontent.com/pod-product-compliance
Lightning Source LLC
Chambersburg PA
CBHW060158050426
42446CB00013B/2885